Great Artists

Georges Seurat

By Iain Zaczek

Gareth Stevens
PUBLISHING

Please visit our website, www.garethstevens.com. For a free color catalog of all our high-quality books, call toll-free 1-800-542-2595 or fax 1-877-542-2596.

Library of Congress Cataloging-in-Publication Data

Zaczek, Iain.
Georges Seurat / by Iain Zaczek.
p. cm. — (Great artists)
Includes index.
ISBN 978-1-4824-1329-8 (pbk.)
ISBN 978-1-4824-1248-2 (6-pack)
ISBN 978-1-4824-1455-4 (library binding)
1. Seurat, Georges, — 1859-1891 — Juvenile literature. 2. Artists — France — Biography — Juvenile literature. I. Zaczek, Iain. II. Title.
ND553.S5 Z33 2015
759.4—d23

Published in 2015 by
Gareth Stevens Publishing
111 East 14th Street, Suite 349
New York, NY 10003

© 2014 Brown Bear Books Ltd

For Brown Bear Books Ltd:
Editorial Director: Lindsey Lowe
Managing Editor: Tim Cooke
Children's Publisher: Anne O'Daly
Design Manager: Keith Davis
Designer: Supriya Sahai
Picture Manager: Sophie Mortimer

Contents

Life Story

The French painter Georges Seurat was very interested in color. He tried a new way of painting. He used lots of dots to create his colors.

Georges-Pierre Seurat was born in Paris on December 2, 1859. His father, Antoine-Chrysostome, was a legal official. He made so much money that he was able to retire early, but he did not spend much time with his family. He lived mainly at their second home outside Paris. Georges only saw his father once a week, on Tuesday evenings, but Georges grew up to be very like his father. He was secretive and independent. He did not spend much time with other people.

Birth name: **Georges-Pierre Seurat**

Born: **December 2, 1859, Paris, France**

Died: **March 29, 1891, Paris, France**

Nationality: **French**

Field: **Painting**

Movement: **Neo-Impressionism, Post-Impressionism, Pointillism**

Influenced by: **Eugène Delacroix**

Georges Seurat, photographed in 1884

ART SCHOOL Georges studied at the École des Beaux-Arts in Paris. It had been founded in 1648 and taught a traditional way of painting.

In 1875, Georges started taking classes at a drawing school. He made two close friends who later became artists: Edmond Aman-Jean and Ernest Laurent.

In 1878, Georges went to the École des Beaux-Arts. It was the best art school in Paris. He learned to paint in a traditional way. But he was also interested in exploring new ways of painting. In 1879, he saw an exhibition by some young painters called the Impressionists. They were not popular at the time because they painted in a new way. Painters like Claude Monet and Edgar Degas tried painting things as they really looked.

Famous Paintings:
🌳 *A Sunday Afternoon on La Grande Jatte* 1884
🌳 *Bathers at Asnières* 1884
🌳 *The Bridge at Courbevoie* 1887
🌳 *Circus Sideshow* 1887
🌳 *Le Chahut* 1890
🌳 *Young Woman Powdering Herself* 1890

"They see poetry in what I have done. No. I apply my methods, and that is all there is to it."

Around this time, Georges was called to serve in the army for a year. In 1880, he returned to Paris and rented a studio with his friend, Edmond.

Georges was lucky. Because his family was wealthy, he did not need to sell his paintings. He could paint what he liked. Georges did many drawings in black chalk. One was a portrait of Edmond. It was accepted at the Paris Salon. This was an exhibition of the best art in France.

Making a splash

At this time, Georges was reading lots about optics, or the study of sight. He also studied how other painters used colors. He noticed that the French artist Eugène Delacroix put two different colors close to one another, rather than mixing them. That changed the way both colors appeared to a viewer.

DOTTY ABOUT DOTS
Georges studied how colors looked together. He put tiny dots of paint next to each other and studied the effect on the eyes.

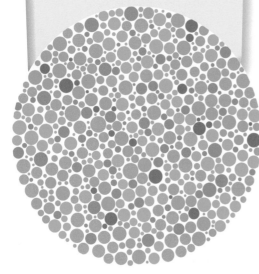

EDMOND AMAN-JEAN
Georges' friend Edmond was a popular French artist. He was famous for pictures of women. He painted *Woman with a Glove* in 1902.

Georges' discoveries would lead him to produce a new kind of painting. It would be very different from what the Salon was used to exhibiting.

In 1883, Georges began to plan a big oil painting. He wanted it to be shown at the Salon. Both Edmond and their friend, Ernest Laurent, had recently had paintings shown at the Salon. Georges painted a riverside scene. It was the kind of subject that was popular with the Impressionists. They liked the effects of light on the water. And they liked painting outdoors.

FRENCH ARMY Georges had to leave art school to do his army service. But he still drew in his free time.

Important people

Edmond Aman-Jean – friend, artist

Ernest Laurent – friend, artist

Paul Signac – friend, artist

Madeleine Knobloch – model, girlfriend

"Great things are done by a series of small things brought together."

Portrait of Paul Signac
by Georges Seurat, 1890

Paul Signac

Georges met the young painter Paul Signac in 1884. Signac began to follow Georges' ideas about color. To begin with, his pictures looked almost the same as Georges'. Signac was more sociable than Georges. He talked to other people about Georges' ideas.

Georges spent a year working on *Bathers at Asnières*. In 1884, the Salon turned it down. Georges was upset. He showed the painting at an exhibition by a group called the Independent Artists of Paris. Georges made friends with some of the other artists. One new friend was Paul Signac. He became a supporter of Georges' techniques.

Final success

Georges started another huge painting. It was called *A Sunday Afternoon on the Island of La Grande Jatte*. It took him nearly two years to finish. He made many drawings of people and other details before he put them all together.

In 1886, Georges included the painting in an exhibition with the Impressionists. Some people criticized the picture.

Painting is the art of hollowing a surface.

But other people believed the painting was a new movement in painting. They called the new movement Neo-Impressionism, or New Impressionism. When Georges' painting was shown at another exhibition, it caused a sensation. So many people crowded around it that no one else could get near it!

GEORGES MET other artists in cafés in Paris. Although he was very shy, he made some good friends. They talked about painting and color.

Tragic end

Soon other artists were copying Georges' style. He did not want to share his secrets. He even thought about keeping his paintings away from exhibitions so that other artists could not copy him.

COLOR STUDIES Georges studied color and light. He kept trying to find new ways to paint until his death.

In March 1891, Georges was helping to prepare an exhibition when he got a sore throat. Doctors did not know what was wrong with him. But his health got much worse. He died on March 29, 1891. He was only 31 years old.

How Seurat Painted

Georges is often called a Neo-Impressionist. He borrowed some ideas from the Impressionists. But he had his own thoughts about color.

Like the Impressionists, Georges liked painting scenes of modern life in Paris. But he wanted to take a more organized approach. He developed a system called pointillism. He put tiny dots of color side by side. Seen from a distance, the colors looked as if they were shimmering. They looked more lively than if the paints had been mixed on the palette.

Dot-by-Dot

Georges put dots of color next to each other. Many other painters, like the Serbian artist Skineta Splajn in her painting of houses, have used the same technique.

OVERVIEW At a distance, the dots merge into a picture we can identify.

CLOSE-UP Tiny patches of the painting just look like random dots.

Georges was also organized in other ways. Before he began a big project, he made numerous sketches from "life." But he always completed his paintings in the studio. The Impressionists tried to capture a brief moment of time. Georges did not. His figures appear solid and constant.

Georges wanted to find new ways of creating moods and emotions in his paintings. He was still trying new experiments with color when he died.

GEORGES BELIEVED that colors mixed together on an artist's palette were not as brilliant as colors that were mixed "in the eye."

A Sunday Afternoon on La Grande Jatte

This is the painting that made Georges famous. He began painting it in 1884. It is huge. He had to stand on a ladder to paint the parts at the top.

La Grande Jatte is a small island in the Seine River. Parisians liked to go there for a walk or a picnic. The people are wearing their best clothes. The picture has an unreal quality. Georges wanted it to look a bit like a frieze from ancient Greece or Egypt. He later added more dots of color.

In the Frame

🔖 The original painting of *A Sunday Afternoon on La Grande Jatte* is 81.7 inches (207.6 cm) tall and 121.25 inches (308 cm) wide.

🔖 The 1984 musical *Sunday in the Park with George* by Stephen Sondheim is based on this painting.

This man seems too small compared with the figure lying next to him. There are other parts of the picture where the size of things seems unreal.

Some people said that Georges' figures looked like dolls. These two men stand stiffly like toy soldiers.

Only the child in the middle of the picture faces directly toward us.

Georges used shadows at the front to lead the eye into the brighter background. This creates a more 3D effect.

SEURAT'S

Palette of the picture

13

Bathers at Asnières

This was Georges' first masterpiece. He created it in 1884. He had not yet fully developed his pointillist style. He later retouched parts of the picture in the new style.

The picture shows workmen relaxing next to the Seine River. Asnières is on the edge of Paris. It has factories and businesses. The Impressionists often painted figures that look sketchy. Georges' bathers seem solid, like statues. They are also all painted in profile, or from the side. Georges later added dots of color to strengthen the originals.

SEURAT'S
Palette of the picture

In the Frame

🍃 The original painting of *Bathers at Asnières* is 79 inches (201 cm) tall and 118 inches (300 cm) wide.

🍃 Georges made many sketches before he painted this huge picture.

> I liked to paint people as quite solid figures.

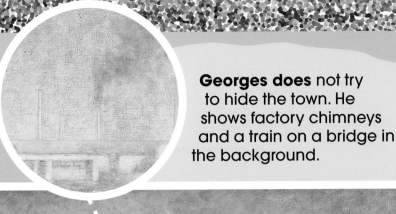

Georges does not try to hide the town. He shows factory chimneys and a train on a bridge in the background.

This small ferryboat flies the French flag. The same boat can also be seen in Georges' painting of La Grande Jatte, pages 12–13.

Painting figures in profile (side-on) was unusual at the time. Georges may have gotten the idea from looking at the art of ancient Egypt.

There is a feeling of heat and stillness. Only this boy cups his hands to make a noise. Is this what makes the little dog on the left jerk its head around?

The Maria, Honfleur

Georges loved to paint the French coast. He visited the port of Honfleur in June 1886. He wanted to try more paintings in his new style.

Georges' pointillist painting of La Grande Jatte had been a big success when it was exhibited that year. While he was at the seaside, Georges decided he did not want to paint the pretty old town of Honfleur. Instead he painted the harbor. The *Maria* was a British cargo ship. It carried wood, coal, and iron to France. It carried farming produce, passengers, and mail back to Britain.

In the Frame

💬 The original painting of *The Maria, Honfleur* is 20.9 inches (53 cm) tall and 25.2 inches (64 cm) wide.

💬 Seurat painted a number of pictures of Honfleur and its harbor.

💬 Other artists also painted this town, including Claude Monet.

The scene is painted from a very low perspective, or viewpoint. This gives it a feeling of unreality.

Georges painted Honfleur many times. Here he used his pointillist technique. He even added a painted border of tiny, colored dots.

The *Maria* carried passengers, cargo, and mail. This sign says the ship sails between Honfleur and London, via Southampton.

Georges chose to show ordinary, working parts of the harbor. This is part of a railroad track used to carry goods along the quay.

SEURAT'S

Palette of the picture

Circus Sideshow

This painting marked a change for Georges. It was his first nighttime scene. He painted it in 1887. The darkness is lit by gaslights.

The painting shows musicians at a circus. They are playing outside the circus tent to attract people to buy tickets for the show inside. This was a real show at a circus in Paris. Georges painted the musicians in simple poses. He divided the background into equal sections going up and down or from one side to the other.

Seurat combined colors such as dashes of blue and pink to show the effects of the lighting on the tree branches.

SEURAT'S

Palette of the picture

In the Frame

🎨 The original painting of *Circus Sideshow* is 39.4 inches (100 cm) tall and 59 inches (150 cm) wide.

🎨 The original French title of the painting is *La Parade*.

Georges planned the picture carefully. The trombone player is exactly at the center of the picture.

This musician is close to the gaslights. They are so bright his face looks bleached out.

The audience is in shadow. Their heads are just dark shapes. The different assorted hats add a kind of border to the foreground (at the front).

19

Le Chahut (Cancan)

The facial features all turn upward. The mouths go up at the sides, like the mustaches of the men. The eyes are also an upward brushstroke.

Georges kept trying new techniques in his paintings. In his later works, he also tried new ways of using lines in his compositions. He painted this picture in 1890.

Some people thought that the direction of the lines in a painting could suggest different moods. Georges tested the idea. He wanted to create a sense of fun. He tried using a series of lines that slanted diagonally upward. The "chahut" was a lively dance. The high kicks of the dancers formed strong diagonal lines.

In the Frame

🖌 The original painting of *Le Chahut* is 67.5 inches (171.5 cm) tall and 55.3 inches (140.5 cm) wide.

🖌 Seurat was fascinated by circuses and theater shows.

🖌 This painting is like posters used to advertise events in Paris at the time.

SEURAT'S

Palette of the picture

The scene is painted from the back of a stage. The audience is seen looking up at the dancers. Georges borrowed the idea from a poster by the artist Jules Chéret.

The bottom of the man's tailcoat and the bows on the women's shoulder straps fly up in exactly the same position.

The angle of the instruments echo the diagonal lines of the dancers' legs.

Young Woman Powdering Herself

This is the only picture that shows us a part of Georges' private life. The woman is his girlfriend, Madeleine Knobloch, in 1890. Georges' family did not know he had a girlfriend.

Georges planned to include a portrait of himself here. But he replaced it with a vase of flowers. It doesn't look as if it belongs in the picture.

Some people think Georges was making fun of Madeleine in this picture. It does not make her look very pretty. She is using a powder puff to put talcum on her skin. She is squeezed into a tight corset. She is sitting at a very small table, which makes her look very big. But Madeleine did not think Georges was teasing her. She was very happy with the painting.

The pale dots around the woman's hand may be part of the pointillist style. But they could also be specks of powder from the powder puff.

In the Frame

🌿 The original painting of *Young Woman Powdering Herself* is 37.1 inches (94.2 cm) tall and 31.3 inches (79.5 cm) wide.

🌿 After Seurat died, Madeleine Knobloch kept this painting for herself.

🌿 The original painting is now in the Courtauld Gallery, London, UK.

The dots of paint can make objects appear less solid. The bow on the mirror blends into the pattern of the wallpaper.

Palette of the picture

Georges uses lines that copy each other. The legs of the mirror and the underside of the table are like the shape of the woman's skirt.

The Circus

This was Georges' last great painting. He started it in 1890. He never quite finished it, but it was exhibited shortly before he died.

This was one of Georges' experiments with line and color. He set it in a circus named the Cirque Fernando. Georges painted the audience to look like cartoon characters. They have comic smiles to show that they are happy. The painting puzzled viewers. They did not really like it. One critic said it was not like art. It was more like a mathematical drawing. After Georges died, the picture was bought by his friend Paul Signac.

Georges copied the pose of the rider and the clown doing a backflip. They appeared in posters by the artist Jules Chéret. Georges liked his work.

Georges used three main colors on a white canvas. He used red for this clown and the ring, yellow for the rider and the other clown, and blue for the audience and the musicians.

In the Frame

The original painting *The Circus* is 72.8 inches (185 cm) tall and 59.8 inches (152 cm) wide.

The man with the beard is the artist Charles Angrand. He was a friend of Georges and a founder of the Society of Independent Artists.

Georges put great movement into this swirling scene, with the clown's streamer and the ringmaster's long, snaking whip.

SEURAT'S

Palette of the picture

What Came Next?

Many young artists wanted to try Georges' pointillist style. They became known as Neo-Impressionists ("New Impressionists").

Many painters tried painting like Georges. Most of them soon gave up. Creating a picture from tiny dots of color was very slow. Some artists felt that thinking about the colors of the dots stopped them painting freely. They were worried that their pictures would become dull.

Famous Neo-Impressionists

- Paul Signac
- Charles Angrand
- Maximilien Luce
- Henri-Edmond Cross
- Albert Dubois-Pillet
- Théo van Rysselberghe
- Camille Pissarro
- Georges Lemmen

Maximilien Luce
Steelworks near Charleroi, 1897

The Impressionist painter Camille Pissarro experimented with Georges' style, but the process was too slow for him. After 4 years, Pissarro went back to his Impressionist style.

THE ORCHARD in Pissarro's picture seems to shimmer in the bright sunlight.

Camille Pissarro
Woman in an Orchard, 1887

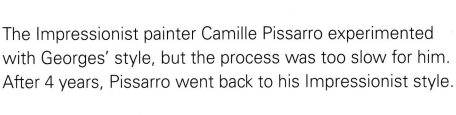

But Georges had a lasting effect on some very important artists. They included Paul Signac, Vincent van Gogh, Paul Gauguin, and Henri Matisse. These painters did not just copy Georges. They used his ideas about color and line to paint in their own way.

Georges often painted deserted ports and harbors. The scenes are so still they do not seem real. This strange feeling was later used in a kind of painting called Surrealism.

How to Paint Like Seurat

Painting with dots might sound a bit dotty. But Georges showed that you can create lovely pictures this way. And dot painting is a lot of fun.

WHAT YOU'LL NEED:

- a photograph (to copy)
- thick white paper or cardboard
- a pencil
- small brushes
- acrylic paints

1.

Choose what to paint. You could try an object or people. You might want to copy a photograph.

2.

Use a pencil to draw the outlines of your picture. Remember that Georges used simple shapes. Look for lines that all go in the same direction.

3.

Make a color wheel. Draw a circle on another piece of paper. Divide the circle into six equal triangles. Fill one triangle with red dots. Leave a triangle white, and fill the next with blue dots. Leave another white triangle and fill the next with yellow dots. Now fill each of the white triangles with dots of the two colors on either side of it.

4.

Look at the triangles of the color wheel where the dots are mixed. When colors are next to one another or overlapping, they make different colors!

5.

Use what you have learned from the color wheel to color in your drawing. Putting dots next to one another will make it look as if the colors are mixed. Stand back from the painting as you work, to see how the picture looks from further away.

6.

Continue until you have filled in all your shapes. Don't rush! It takes time to paint all the dots. Make sure you let the different parts of the painting dry before you add a new color.

Timeline

1859: Born in Paris, France.

1875: Goes to drawing school.

1878: Studies at the École des Beaux-Arts in Paris.

1879: Sees an exhibition of paintings by the Impressionists.

1880: Opens a studio in Paris with Edmond Aman-Jean.

1881: Begins to study optics.

1883: Begins work on *Bathers at Asnières*.

1884: *Bathers at Asnières* is turned down by the Paris Salon.

1886: Exhibits *A Sunday Afternoon on La Grande Jatte*, which causes a sensation.

1891: Dies suddenly in Paris.

Glossary

composition: How a picture is put together from separate elements.

foreground: The part of a picture that is closest to the viewer.

frieze: A horizontal band of painting or carvings that goes across a wall.

Impressionist: One of a group of artists who tried to show objects as they appeared at a first glance.

Neo-Impressionist: A style of painting. Its name means "New Impressionism."

optics: The study of sight and light and how people see things.

Pointillism: A style of painting using tiny dots of individual colors that become mixed together in the eye of the viewer.

profile: A view of someone or something seen from the side.

sensation: A reaction of great interest and excitement.

Surrealism: A style of painting that showed strange and dreamlike subjects.

symmetry: The way the parts of a picture reflect each another.

traditional: Something that has been done in the same way for a long time.

Further information

BOOKS

Burleigh, Robert. *Seurat and La Grande Jatte: Connecting the Dots*. Harry N. Abrams, 2004.

Cassidy, Jacqueline. *The Primary Kids Meet Georges Seurat*. Primary Media Inc., 2010.

Cesar, Stanley. *Twenty Georges-Pierre Seurat Paintings (Collection) for Kids*. Kindle edition, 2013.

Sabbeth, Carole. *Monet and the Impressionists for Kids: Their Lives and Ideas, 21 Activities*. Chicago Review Press, 2002.

Venezia, Mike, and Milk Venezia. *Georges Seurat* (Getting to Know the World's Great Artists). Children's Press, 2002.

MUSEUMS

You can see Georges' famous paintings from this book in these museums:

A Sunday Afternoon on La Grande Jatte
Art Institute of Chicago

Bathers at Asnières
National Gallery, London, UK

The Maria, Honfleur
National Gallery, Prague, Czech Republic

Circus Sideshow
Metropolitan Museum of Art, New York City

Le Chahut
Kröller-Müller Museum, Otterlo, Netherlands

Young Woman Powdering Herself
Courtauld Gallery, London, UK

The Circus
Musée d'Orsay, Paris, France

WEBSITES

http://www.georgesseurat.org/
A huge site that includes a gallery of all of Georges' paintings.

http://makingartfun.com/htm/f-maf-art-library/georges-seurat-biography.htm
"Meet Georges Seurat" page from Art Library, with links to projects.

http://www.howstuffworks.com/arts/artwork/paintings-by-georges-seurat.htm
A guide to Georges and his works from How Stuff Works.

http://www.ducksters.com/biography/artists/georges_seurat.php
An introduction to Georges from the Ducksters website, with fascinating facts.

Index